EXPLORING THE STATES

Tennessee

THE VOLUNTEER STATE

by Amy Rechner

BLASTOFF! 5 READERS

BELLWETHER MEDIA • MINNEAPOLIS, MN

Note to Librarians, Teachers, and Parents:

Blastoff! Readers are carefully developed by literacy experts and combine standards-based content with developmentally appropriate text.

Level 1 provides the most support through repetition of high-frequency words, light text, predictable sentence patterns, and strong visual support.

Level 2 offers early readers a bit more challenge through varied simple sentences, increased text load, and less repetition of high-frequency words.

Level 3 advances early-fluent readers toward fluency through increased text and concept load, less reliance on visuals, longer sentences, and more literary language.

Level 4 builds reading stamina by providing more text per page, increased use of punctuation, greater variation in sentence patterns, and increasingly challenging vocabulary.

Level 5 encourages children to move from "learning to read" to "reading to learn" by providing even more text, varied writing styles, and less familiar topics.

Whichever book is right for your reader, Blastoff! Readers are the perfect books to build confidence and encourage a love of reading that will last a lifetime!

This edition first published in 2014 by Bellwether Media, Inc.

No part of this publication may be reproduced in whole or in part without written permission of the publisher. For information regarding permission, write to Bellwether Media, Inc., Attention: Permissions Department, 5357 Penn Avenue South, Minneapolis, MN 55419.

Library of Congress Cataloging-in-Publication Data

Rechner, Amy.
Tennessee / by Amy Rechner.
    pages cm. – (Blastoff! readers. Exploring the States)
Summary: "Developed by literacy experts for students in grades three through seven, this book introduces young readers to the geography and culture of Tennessee"– Provided by publisher.
Includes bibliographical references and index.
ISBN 978-1-62617-042-1 (hardcover : alk. paper)
1. Tennessee–Juvenile literature. I. Title.
F436.3.R43 2014
976.8–dc23

2013011514

Printed in the United States of America, North Mankato, MN.

Table of Contents

Where Is Tennessee?

Missouri

Kentucky

Nashville ★

Mississippi River

Arkansas

Tennessee

● Memphis

Mississippi

Alabama

Tennessee is a narrow state in the middle of the eastern United States. Kentucky and Virginia share Tennessee's northern border. North Carolina lies to the east. Georgia, Alabama, and Mississippi make up the state's southern border. The Mississippi River separates Tennessee from its western neighbors, Arkansas and Missouri.

Virginia

Knoxville •

Craighead
Caverns

Cumberland
Caverns

North
Carolina

N

W   E

S

Chattanooga

Georgia

The forest-covered ridges of the Great Smoky Mountains run between Tennessee and North Carolina. Their ancient peaks rise high above the state. The city of Memphis is in Tennessee's southwest corner. The state capital of Nashville is near the center of the state.

History

The Cherokee and Chickasaw **Native** Americans were living in Tennessee when Spanish explorers arrived in 1540. The French built a settlement in 1682. Great Britain took control of Tennessee after the French and Indian Wars. It lost the land after **colonists** won the **Revolutionary War**. Tennessee became the sixteenth state in 1796.

fun fact

Tennessean Andrew Jackson was the seventh U.S. President. He was a famous general during the War of 1812.

Tennessee Timeline!

1540: Hernando de Soto of Spain is the first European to explore Tennessee.

1673: French explorers Jacques Marquette and Louis Joliet arrive near Memphis. British explorers cross the mountains into eastern Tennessee.

1763: Great Britain takes control of land west of the thirteen colonies.

1796: Tennessee becomes the sixteenth state.

1838-1839: The U.S. government forces the Cherokee and other Native Americans to leave Tennessee. The path they follow west is called the Trail of Tears.

1954: Rock 'n' roll legend Elvis Presley records his first hit song at Sun Studio in Memphis.

1960: African-American teenagers sit at whites-only lunch counters in Nashville. This is to protest laws that separate people by race.

1968: Civil rights leader Martin Luther King, Jr. is killed in Memphis.

1960 sit-in

Marquette and Joliet with Native Americans

Elvis Presley

The Land

Tennessee's land regions vary greatly across the state. The Appalachian Mountains rise along the eastern border. They include the Great Smoky Mountains, one of the world's oldest ranges. The region's **fertile** valleys are good for farming. Farther west, the Cumberland **Plateau** features flat-topped mountains.

The land slopes down into the Central **Basin** in the middle of the state. Its rolling grasslands are home to grazing cattle. In the west is the **Gulf** Coastal Plain. This flat, swampy region falls between the Tennessee and Mississippi Rivers. Its rich soil is perfect for growing crops.

fun fact

Reelfoot Lake in northwest Tennessee was created by a series of earthquakes in the early 1800s.

Reelfoot Lake

Great Smoky Mountains

Tennessee's Climate

average °F

spring
Low: 48°
High: 70°

summer
Low: 67°
High: 88°

fall
Low: 50°
High: 71°

winter
Low: 31°
High: 50°

Caves

Mystery Falls

Did you know?
Mystery Falls is the deepest pit in Tennessee. It reaches 281 feet (86 meters) below the earth!

A network of more than 9,000 caves lies below Tennessee's soil. Water flowed underground for millions of years to carve out these dark spaces. The Cumberland **Caverns** is a famous string of caves. It boasts a waterfall, deep pools, and stunning rock formations.

Craighead Caverns

Ruby Falls

fun fact

Ruby Falls is a large underground waterfall. It plunges 145 feet (44 meters) inside a cave within Lookout Mountain.

Craighead Caverns contains the Lost Sea. This is the largest underground lake in the country. Scientists are still not sure how deep the lake is. Divers have found water-filled caves below the lake's surface. On the way to the lake, visitors admire spiky formations called "cave flowers." These crystal clusters form in only a few of the world's caves.

Wildlife

Tennessee's wilderness shelters many kinds of wildlife. Deer, bobcats, and coyotes roam the state. Raccoons and rabbits search for food in the woodlands. Wild hogs live in the mountains and the Cumberland Plateau. Wildflowers like bluebells and false indigo color the mountains and the plateau.

Elm, beech, cedar, and fir trees fill the state's forests. Eagles, hawks, and owls hunt for prey overhead. Songbirds dart among the treetops. Loons, grebes, and herons feed along rivers filled with perch and catfish.

false indigo

grebe

wild hog

albino deer

**Tennessee
State Capitol**

The rich history and natural beauty of Tennessee draw visitors to the state. People experience Appalachian culture at the Dollywood amusement park in Pigeon Forge. Many others hike the long, winding mountain paths of Great Smoky Mountains National Park. Its peaks draw many visitors to the national park every year.

Nashville boasts plenty of landmarks. The Tennessee State **Capitol** stands proudly on a hill overlooking the city. History fans explore the state throughout the ages at the Tennessee State Museum. They can also tour the magnificent mansion that was once home to President Andrew Jackson.

Lookout Mountain

fun fact
Lookout Mountain stands tall near the border with Georgia. It is said that on a clear day, visitors can see seven states from the peak.

Memphis

Memphis's location on the Mississippi River helped it grow in the 1800s. Southern farmers sent their cotton crops up the river to Memphis to sell. Today, the city's Cotton Museum explores the history of the cotton trade. Nearby, the National **Civil Rights** Museum tells the story of the African-American struggle for equality. It is built around the Lorraine Motel, where Martin Luther King, Jr. was killed.

The famous Sun Studio is also in Memphis. Many famous artists recorded there, including Johnny Cash, Jerry Lee Lewis, and Elvis Presley. Presley's home of Graceland is another popular **tourist** stop. More than a half-million people visit this Memphis site each year.

Did you know?

Musicians come from all over the world to visit Gibson Guitars in Nashville. This company is known for its Les Paul electric guitars.

Many Tennesseans have **service jobs**. They work in hospitals, schools, and government centers. Others serve tourists at hotels and restaurants. Factory workers make food products, vehicles, and chemicals. Miners dig for crushed rock, zinc, and coal. Fishers harvest mussels from the Tennessee River.

Workers haul lumber from the state's forests. Farmers grow cotton, tobacco, soybeans, and corn. They also raise livestock such as chicken, hogs, and horses. The Tennessee walking horse is a special breed used for riding and in horse shows.

Where People Work in Tennessee

manufacturing
10%

farming and
natural resources
3%

government
12%

services
75%

Playing

There is a lot of outdoor fun to be had in beautiful Tennessee. White-water rafting is popular on the Pigeon River near Gatlinburg. Mountain hiking and **caving** offer excitement in eastern Tennessee. Water lovers can fish, boat, and kayak on Reelfoot Lake and Tennessee's many rivers. Hunters search for **game** across the state.

fishing

NASCAR
Speed Park

! fun fact

When they feel the need for speed, Tennesseans head to the NASCAR Speed Park in Sevierville. They can race on small tracks to experience the thrill of a real NASCAR race.

Live music is a big part of Tennessee culture. Bands play nightly in every major city and many small towns. Music lovers enjoy **blues**, country, **bluegrass**, and **gospel**. Rock concerts attract fans to the state's larger cities and music festivals. The Tennessee Theater in Knoxville hosts plays, concerts, and dance performances.

Chocolate Fried Pies

Ingredients:

1/2 cup sugar

2 tablespoons cocoa powder

4 tablespoons butter

1/3 cup flour

1 cup evaporated milk

1 teaspoon vanilla

1 premade pie crust, unbaked

Oil for frying

Directions:

1. Combine sugar, cocoa powder, butter, flour, evaporated milk, and vanilla. Cook on medium heat, stirring constantly until thickened. Let cool.

2. Roll out pie crust on a floured surface to 1/4 of an inch. Cut into 6-inch rounds. (Empty cans work well as cutters.)

3. Center 2 to 3 tablespoons of filling on each round. Then fold over and seal using a fork.

4. Heat oil in a large skillet on medium heat. Fry pies to a golden brown, turning once.

Note: Any other pie filling can easily be substituted for a different flavor of pie!

fried chicken

stack cake

The big flavors and portions of Southern cooking are popular in Tennessee. Ham, cornbread, and greens often show up on dinner tables. Memphis is famous for its unique barbecue style called dry rub. Spices and herbs are rubbed on meat before it is smoked or grilled. Fried catfish is another Memphis favorite. Spicy fried chicken heats up taste buds in Nashville.

Southern desserts include pecan pie and crispy filled pastries called fried pies. Stack cake is a **traditional** wedding cake in the South. Jam or dried fruit is spread between thin layers of cake to make this treat. Milk, Tennessee's state beverage, washes it all down.

23

Festivals

There is always something to celebrate in Tennessee. The Beale Street Music Festival in Memphis is three days of live rock, pop, and blues concerts. The Country Music Association hosts the CMA Music Festival in Nashville every June. Country music stars and new artists perform on three outdoor stages. The Bonnaroo Music and Arts Festival is a four-day event held in Manchester, Tennessee.

CMA
Music Festival

Jonesborough hosts the National Storytelling Festival in October. Thousands of people come to listen to stories of all kinds. Uncle Dave Macon Days in Murfreesboro celebrates old Tennessee music and dance. Banjo music, **clog dancing**, and more keep Tennessee culture alive.

Great American Music

Tennessee music has inspired thousands of musicians. Smoky Mountain bluegrass and Memphis blues are rooted in Tennessee. Gospel, country, and rock 'n' roll also have important ties to the state.

Nashville is home to the Country Music Hall of Fame and the Grand Ole Opry radio show. The Grand Ole Opry has aired weekly since the 1920s. It brought country music to national attention. Memphis's Beale Street is lined with blues music clubs. The Memphis Rock 'n' Soul Museum explores the history of music in Memphis. Great music continues to make Tennessee a lively and colorful state.

Beale Street

Fast Facts About Tennessee

Tennessee's Flag

The flag of Tennessee is bright red with a circle in the center. The circle is blue with a white border. Inside it are three white stars, one for each distinct land region of the state. Blue and white stripes mark the flag's right edge.

State Flower
iris

State Nicknames:	The Volunteer State The Big Bend State
State Motto:	"Agriculture and Commerce"
Year of Statehood:	1796
Capital City:	Nashville
Other Major Cities:	Memphis, Knoxville, Chattanooga
Population:	6,346,105 (2010)
Area:	42,145 square miles (109,155 square kilometers); Tennessee is the 36th largest state.
Major Industries:	farming, manufacturing, tourism, mining
Natural Resources:	limestone, zinc, coal, farmland, lumber, water systems
State Government:	99 representatives; 33 senators
Federal Government:	9 representatives; 2 senators
Electoral Votes:	11

State Animal
raccoon

State Bird
northern mockingbird

Glossary

basin—an area of land that is lower than the surrounding land

bluegrass—a type of music that features banjos, mandolins, fiddles, and harmonious vocals

blues—a style of folk music that originated among African-American musicians in the South

capitol—the building in which state representatives and senators meet

caverns—caves made of rock that dissolves in water over time; caverns feature a variety of rock formations.

caving—cave exploring

civil rights—the rights of people to receive equal treatment under the laws of a country

clog dancing—a dance form in which performers beat out the rhythms with their feet

colonists—people who settle new land for their home country

fertile—able to support growth

game—wild animals that are hunted for food or sport

gospel—a type of music often characterized by songs of praise, strong vocals, and repetition

gulf—part of an ocean or sea that extends into land

native—originally from a specific place

plateau—an area of flat, raised land

Revolutionary War—the war between 1775 and 1783 in which the United States fought for independence from Great Britain

service jobs—jobs that perform tasks for people or businesses

tourist—a person who travels to visit another place

traditional—relating to a custom, idea, or belief handed down from one generation to the next

To Learn More

AT THE LIBRARY
Edgers, Geoff. *Who Was Elvis Presley?* New York, N.Y.: Grosset & Dunlap, 2007.

Gosman, Gillian. *Martin Luther King Jr.* New York, N.Y.: PowerKids Press, 2011.

Somervill, Barbara A. *Tennessee*. New York, N.Y.: Children's Press/Scholastic, 2010.

ON THE WEB
Learning more about Tennessee is as easy as 1, 2, 3.

1. Go to www.factsurfer.com.

2. Enter "Tennessee" into the search box.

3. Click the "Surf" button and you will see a list of related Web sites.

With factsurfer.com, finding more information is just a click away.

Index